THE MELTING POT: AMERICA IS LOST WITHOUT IT

America has long been known as a great melting pot in which people of various ethnic heritages and cultures have melted into a common American culture and national identity. We are a nation wherein the collective contributions of people of various ethnic, cultural, and religious backgrounds have imparted unique values, ideals, work ethic, culture, a fervent desire to succeed, and a national patriotism that recognizes the importance of the good of the nation as a whole over that of the individual in times of crisis. We saw ourselves as a melting pot for the first two hundred years of our history. Then, in the late twentieth century societal elites and political activists began challenging the melting pot concept claiming that the assimilation of people into a common American culture was an unfair subjection of members of other races and cultures. These multiculturists want to preserve immigrant cultures and native languages rather than absorb American culture.

Could the United States successfully exist as a multicultural nation? Our national identity is derived from our common culture and values. We derive our national interests from our national identity. Our national interests are manifested in our national political ideology and national policies, and in turn in our National Security Strategy. Would Americans be willing to pledge their lives, their fortunes, and their national honor in the pursuit of national interests if our national identity depended upon a consensus derived from negotiations and compromises between competing ethnic groups?

The answer to these questions, in my opinion, is no. We are the great nation and world hegemonic power today because of our melting pot. Our melting pot created a society in which our national identity is founded in our common culture and our civic creed. Should multiculturism prevail and we no longer assimilate newcomers into our American culture, then we risk the disintegration of our national identity. If we lose our national identity then our national political ideology, national policies, and national security are no longer sustainable.

The backbone of the United States rests in the Declaration of Independence and in the U.S. Constitution. The principles contained in these documents, combined with the collective contributions of people of various ethnic, cultural, and religious backgrounds, are what have made this country great. Our American identity is reflected in our common culture and civic creed. We derive our culture from the values and institutions of our original settlers. They imparted a common language and traditions of the separation of church and state, and the value of the individual in society. We as Americans believe in equality among men, women, and among different cultural heritages. We also recognize that while our culture may change over time, it retains continuity. We derive our creed from a set of universal ideas and principles contained within our founding documents authored by our first leaders. They include liberty, equality, democracy, constitutionalism, liberalism, limited government, and private enterprise.[1]

In 1790, newly elected President George Washington wrote a letter to a Jewish congregation in response to their letter congratulating him on his election to the presidency. He used the letter as an opportunity to put forth his vision of America. He wrote: "It is now that tolerance is no more spoken of, as if it was by the indulgence of one class of people, that another enjoyed the exercise of their inherent natural rights. For happily the government of the United States, which gives to bigotry no sanction, to persecution no assistance, requires only that they who live under its protection should demean themselves as good citizens, in giving it on all occasions their effectual support."[2]

President Washington's statement describes the idea of the melting pot long before we created the concept. In his vision of our new, fledgling nation anyone could become an American. America would accept them regardless of background and treat them as an equal. This nation would not be monoethnic, but a multiethnic nation of a common culture and creed. Washington provided a good working formula for assimilating tens of millions of immigrants who would come to America. "They would be eligible for citizenship, entitled to be treated as an equal to every other American, provided they accepted civic obligations and the civic culture."[3]

Most of us were taught about the melting pot in school while growing up. The melting pot is a metaphor for a heterogeneous society becoming more homogeneous, the different elements melting together into a harmonious whole with a common culture. The "melting together" into a harmonious whole refers to the accepting of the common values and ideals that identify us as Americans. However, it does not refer to a loss of ethnic identity. In fact, it is the uniqueness of the different ethnic cultures that contributed to the American identity that has made this country so strong, and why it is critically important to the future success of this country.

The very fabric of our great country is weaved from the diverse cultures of the various groups of people who came to this country. Over time, the respective strengths and character of these diverse peoples melted into the very qualities and values that we as Americans cherish. Yet, the identities of these respective contributing cultures did not melt away. Indeed, they were not lost. Jewish Americans, Italian Americans, Irish Americans, German Americans, Polish Americans, African Americans, Latin Americans, Asian Americans, etc. are all distinctly recognizable not simply by their physical characteristics or religion, but also by their unique cultural qualities. America is far from a culturally or ethnically homogeneous society. But all these cultures and ethnicities have changed the culture of America.

Today, the majority of Americans have at least one ancestor who immigrated to this country sometime after the mid-nineteenth century. By the definitions of race in existence in 1900, we are a nation consisting of a majority of minorities. Nevertheless we are still a recognizably American nation. "Although modern U.S. society considers people of Irish, Italian, Polish, and English descent "white," in 1911 these four European nationalities were considered separate "races"."[4] The descendants of these immigrants who were considered to be of different races in 1900 have now become deeply interwoven into the fabric of American life. It is impossible to envision what America would be like without them.[5]

In looking back across our history, we can recognize that the U.S. has in fact never been a monoethnic nation. The original colonies were settled by distinctly different groups of people from different parts of the British Isles, each having unique culture in terms of religion, politics, and different customs and behaviors. Similarly, German immigrants who settled in Pennsylvania had their own distinctive cultural traditions and religion. Today, we consider all of these different groups of people to be part of the American majority. Yet, each group imparted very different and valuable aspects of their heritage and cultures upon our American identity.

Immigration in the nineteenth and early twentieth centuries significantly influenced our national culture. Their collective work ethic, sacrifices, and ingenuity fueled the industrialization and expansion of America. The continued immigration to the United States has allowed this country to maintain a growing population which in turn allows for continued economic growth. "The Wall Street Journal calls for high levels of immigration because it means more consumers, more workers, and a larger economy with new blood for the United States."[6]

Indeed, immigration has made and remade this country. However, the great benefits of immigration can only be realized if we require that our immigrants assimilate into our American culture. Transforming eager immigrants into valuable, productive American citizens can only be achieved through an effective integration and education process that emphasizes mastery of our common language, English, and instills our civic values and beliefs.

America has employed various methodologies and policies for the assimilation of our immigrants over time. Prior to the twentieth century, assimilation "involved an implicit contract in which immigrants were welcomed as equal members of the national community and urged to become citizens, provided they accepted English as the national language and committed themselves to the principles of the American Creed and the Protestant work ethic."[7] In return, immigrants could practice their own folkways as they desired in their homes and local communities.

The large influx of immigrants into large cities such as Boston, New York Philadelphia, and Chicago during the early part of the twentieth century caught the attention of the societal elites of the time. They recognized that these immigrants needed to become part of American society. They should live by its laws, work at jobs, learn English, and earn citizenship. Theodore Roosevelt was one of the foremost advocates. He said in 1915: "We cannot afford to use hundreds of thousands of immigrants merely as industrial assets while they remain social outcasts and menaces any more than fifty years ago we could afford to keep the black man merely as an industrial asset and not as a human being."[8] The result was the development of a program to "Americanize" immigrants wherein they would be taught English, United States history, government, and culture as part of their integration into American society.

We, as a nation, didn't always get it right in assimilating our new citizens. At times, immigrants were discriminated against and simultaneously subjected to major programs to incorporate them into the national culture and society. Overall, however, assimilation worked well. Immigration renewed American society; Americanization preserved American culture.[9]

There are countless examples of successful Americans who exemplify our values. They come from all ethnic and cultural backgrounds. They are both men and women. I chose to discuss a few people who represent the broad spectrum of great Americans. None of them were born as American citizens but left an indelible mark on our history: a Catholic saint, an agronomist and chemist, and a diplomat.

Saint Frances Xavier Cabrini was the first American to be canonized as a saint in the Catholic Church. Born in Lombardi, Italy in 1850, she was the youngest of 13 children in a family of cherry tree farmers. She became a nun in 1877. Mother Cabrini, along with six other sisters, founded the Missionary Sisters of the Sacred Heart of Jesus in 1880. Her success with her mission caught the attention of Pope Leo XIII who directed her to go to the United States to help with the Italian immigrants who were flooding to America, many living in poverty.

A remarkable woman endowed with exceptional administrative skills, Mother Cabrini founded orphanages, schools, and hospitals throughout America in the aid of Italian immigrants and children. Her work took her all over the United States and South America. She became a U.S. citizen in 1909, and she died in 1917. In 1946, Pope Pius XII canonized Frances Xavier Cabrini as the patron saint of immigrants, making her the first American saint. [10,11]

George Washington Carver stands out as one of the truly great men of his time. He was an American agricultural chemist, agronomist, and experimenter who almost single-handedly revolutionized southern agriculture. From his small laboratory on the campus of the Tuskegee Normal and Industrial Institute flowed hundreds of discoveries and products from the once neglected peanut and little known sweet potato.

He was born a slave in 1861 on a plantation near Diamond Grove, Missouri. He left the plantation at the age of twelve to pursue an education after being freed from slavery. He acquired a Master of Science degree in 1896. Shortly thereafter, he became the director of the newly organized department of agricultural research at the Tuskegee Normal and Industrial Institute in Tuskegee, Alabama.

George Washington Carver devoted his life to the betterment of his fellow man. His work, originally designed to improve the quality of life for the poor, black sharecroppers, facilitated an enhanced life for the entire South. His efforts brought about significant advances in agricultural training and farming methods in an era when farming was the largest single occupation of Americans. [12,13]

Marie Jana Korbel (Madeleine Albright) was born the daughter of a diplomat in Czechoslovakia in 1937. She and her family escaped Nazi occupation by fleeing to England in 1939. The Korbels returned to Czechoslovakia after World War II, but were forced to flee in 1948 to escape a communist coup. This time, they settled in the United States.

Madeleine Albright attended school and eventually earned her master's degree and doctorate from Columbia University's Department of Public Law and Government. She then transitioned to a very successful career in government. She served as a staff member on the National Security Council, a Senior Fellow at the Center for Strategic Studies, a professor at Georgetown University, and President of the Center for National Policy.

President Bill Clinton named her Ambassador to the United Nations in 1993 in recognition of her professional achievements. As the U.S. Ambassador, Madam Albright earned a reputation for tough-mindedness as a fierce advocate for American interests. Her success as an ambassador eventually led to her nomination and unanimous confirmation by the U.S. Senate in January 1997 as the sixty-forth Secretary of State. She was the first woman to become Secretary of State and she held the position until 2001. [14,15]

Each of these people displayed many of the values that we identify with being uniquely American. Individually, each of these model Americans epitomizes the concept of the melting pot. We must continue to assimilate our newcomers to our great nation in such a way as to continue to develop and strengthen our American culture. We must hold them accountable for contributing to American society by learning English and obtaining an education that includes American history and civics as well as math and science. We must also integrate these immigrants into our American society so that they too may be successful and contribute to the betterment of this nation.

Late twentieth century saw the change in viewpoint of Americanization as being good to that of being discriminatory. The concept of the American melting pot has been taken under scrutiny over the past few decades. Societal elites and political activists challenged the melting pot model claiming that the various cultural differences in society are valuable and should be preserved, not diluted into a homogeneous culture. These multiculturists offered an alternative metaphor of the tossed salad as a better description in that various cultures mix but remain distinct and identifiable. The problem with the tossed salad metaphor is that it creates a sense of separateness; a tendency to focus on the differences between the various ethnic and religious cultures found in our society vice focusing on the commonalities and overarching characteristics and values that make us American.

Unlike those of the early twentieth century, our societal elites of the late twentieth century saw Americanization as an unfair subjection of members of other races and cultures. The solution for the fair treatment of immigrants pursued by the multiculturists was to give them protections of civil rights legislation. This came to mean demanding for the benefits of racial quotas and of government spending programs such as bilingual education, ethnic study programs in colleges and universities, and proportional representation in electoral districts, employment, and in the awarding of official contracts.[16] They desired an America that would be made up of separate and disparate multicultural groups, fenced off in their own communities, entitled to make demands on the larger society but without any responsibility to assimilate to the American way of life.[17]

> The ideologies of multiculturalism and diversity reinforce and legitimatize these trends. They deny the existence of a common culture in the United States, denounce assimilation, and promote the primacy of racial, ethnic, and other subnational cultural identities and groupings. They also question a central element in the American Creed by substituting for the rights of individuals the rights of groups, defined largely in terms of race, ethnicity, gender, and sexual preference.[18]

Although the intentions of the elites and multiculturists to resolve the problems of discrimination among the different ethnicities were admirable, they wrongly attempted to apply a solution for discrimination of race to the problem of immigration and equality. The civil rights movements of the 1960s were necessary and valid for the issue over discrimination of black Americans. However, the issue with immigration has always been assimilation, not discrimination. In fact, when we consider the history of immigration to our country, we realize that ethnic or racial discrimination were not significant obstacles to overcome. The Irish, Italians, and Jews were all initially considered to be of different ethnicities than the Americans at the time, but these groups are now considered to be just as American as anyone else.

The contrast with the past is remarkable. Our Founding Fathers saw diversity as both a reality and a challenge to be dealt with: hence the national motto, *e pluribus unum* – one out of many. They recognized the importance of ingraining in our collective consciousness the overarching ideal of being American regardless of heritage as the key to the longevity of our nation. The current proponents of multiculturism and diversity have been partially successful in dismantling what our Founding Fathers in their wisdom recognized as the foundation of what separates America from other countries. Theodore Roosevelt also recognized the danger of promoting multiculturism over nationalism when he warned: "The one absolutely certain way of bringing this nation to ruin, of preventing all possibility of its continuing as a nation at all, would be to permit it to become a tangle of squabbling nationalities..."[19]

The resultant government policies and fostered administrative practices have retarded the assimilation of immigrants vice progress their assimilation. Bilingual education programs, as an example, were meant to ease the transition into an English speaking culture. However, they achieved the very opposite effect in that they have kept Latino immigrants' children in Spanish-language instruction and denied them the knowledge of English that they need to advance in American society. Alternatively, these children should have been immersed in English speaking classrooms where they would gain a knowledge of English and basic reading and mathematics skills, and an appreciation of the American civic culture. In turn, they would be given a fair chance at being as successful in our society as their abilities will take them.[20]

Contrary to popular belief, bilingual education has not been effective. In fact, many school districts have moved away from bilingual education, and are now placing non-English speaking children in various forms of English immersion instruction. Christine Rossell is a professor of political science at Boston University and the author of *Bilingual Education Reform in Massachusetts* and numerous other studies analyzing the effectiveness of bilingual education programs. Her research indicates that students in general are much more successful at learning a second language as well as subject matter in that second language by learning in the second language rather than learning in the students' native language.[21]

"Despite the common belief in the effectiveness of bilingual education, my observations and my analyses of data from state department of education web sites indicate that only a minority of immigrant children in the United States are enrolled in bilingual programs in any form."[22] After over two decades of bilingual education programs being in existence, many states have turned to alternate, more successful programs for their non-English speaking students. California moved away from bilingual education as the primary approach in 1998. Similarly, Arizona and Massachusetts mandated the use of English immersion programs in 2000 and in 2002, respectively.[23]

In observing almost 200 classrooms in California over a period of five years from 1999 through 2004, Dr. Rossell learned that: "former Spanish bilingual education teachers were impressed by how quickly and eagerly their Spanish-speaking language learners in kindergarten and 1st grade learned to speak and read in English and how proud the students were of this accomplishment. The teachers were also surprised at how much they themselves liked teaching in sheltered English immersion classrooms..."[24]

Dr. Rossell's comprehensive research reinforces the importance of the melting pot approach in assimilating immigrants into our great nation. Kenneth Blackwell, former Mayor of Cincinnati and U.S. Ambassador to the United Nations Human Rights Commission, affirms the results of her study in his comment: "Being fluent in English is essential if you want to succeed in America. Someone who can speak English can compete for better jobs, with better pay. Someone who can speak English improves their chances to have a better future for themselves and their children."[25]

Kenneth Blackwell argues that most Americans disagree with the agendas of many elites and some of the more radical liberal groups who push for legislation that prevents American businesses and organizations from requiring their employees to be able to speak English. He states that nearly ninety percent of Americans think it's very important for immigrants to be able to speak English, and over seventy-five percent believe that employers have the right to require employees to speak English while on the job.[26] "Give a person coddling treatment in his native language, and he'll get through the day. Teach an immigrant, or anyone in this country, how to master the English language, and he can soar on eagle wings to capture the fullest measure of the American dream."[27]

Our neighbor to the North offers a great case study in the difficulties of a multilingual society. Canada is a country of two languages: English and French. The official language in all provinces less Quebec is English. The official language in the province of Quebec is French. The ongoing dispute over the predominance of these two languages at the national level has been detrimental to the Canadian society as a whole.

> In 1995, the predominantly French-speaking province of Quebec came within a few thousand votes of seceding from Canada. The national government must cater to Quebec to preserve order and maintain a cohesive government. This has spurred secessionist movements in English-speaking western Canada on the grounds that the Canadian government favors French speakers. While the policy of official multilingualism has led to disunity, resentment, and near-secession, it is also very costly. Canada's dual-language requirement costs approximately $260 million each year. Canada has one-tenth the population of the United States and spent that amount accommodating only two languages. A

13

similar language policy in the United States would cost much more than $4 billion annually...[28]

In speaking with a Canadian federal government civil service employee, I learned that the government requires all personnel in management level positions to be able to speak both English and French. As a result, the government must pay for language training for these personnel to become proficient in a second language. The consequence of allowing for multiple official languages has been the need for unnecessary and expensive government spending. It has also caused significant tension within the Canadian society to the point of nearly fragmenting the nation into multiple subnations.

The Canadian experience reinforces the American experience as the model for a successful nation. Our successful assimilation of people from multiple heritages, cultures, and languages into one, common civic culture with a common language created the strong economic and international power that is America. Yet, at the same time we've managed to absorb elements of all these cultures into our national identity while allowing for each culture to retain and practice its own religion, traditions and language. "Only in America have a variety of ethnic groups retained their own original cultures, and nobody seems to mind."[29]

American Demographics, a market and demographics research firm conducted a survey regarding how U.S. residents of foreign descent view themselves. Their research revealed that eighty-three percent of the country's residents identify their culture and traditions as being American.[30] The goal of the survey was to determine which Americans associate themselves more closely with the folkways and cultures of their ancestors, and which identify themselves as being American. U.S. residents of

European heritage overwhelmingly view themselves as Americans. Ninety percent of both Eastern and Western European descendents claim to be culturally American A majority of residents of Latin American, African, and Middle Eastern heritage also see their traditions as essentially American.[31] "Of course, many Americans identify with their Italian, African, or Asian roots. Cultural diversity is what makes this country so unique...But in terms of our day-to-day lives, we act like...well, Americans."[32]

In America today, we have more young adults of Latin or Asian descent and foreign-born than at any other time in our history. What affect will this new generation of immigrants have on the strength of our national identity? Faria Chideya, an award winning journalist and author of *The Color of Our Future,* explains "we're in a transitional phase right now where foreign influences are going to be seen as 'Latin American,' 'Asian American,' and on...But eventually, they'll be identified as simply 'American.'"[33] She goes on to claim that these new foreign influences are already being woven into our American culture. Faria Chideya uses the example of salsa recently outselling ketchup for the first time to make her point. "Is salsa American? It is now," she says. She further argues that it is not about whether the foreign influences will dilute the strength of our national identity but "which cultural influences will stick and become part of the larger American culture?"[34]

Although our efforts over the course of time to assimilate the multiple cultures that make up America have not been without error, they have been extremely successful. We have also learned from our mistakes, and we are a better nation because of this. The melting pot created a society that views itself as having a national identity. Our American identity is founded in our culture and in our creed. Americans believe in the separation of church and state, and in the value of the individual in society. We also believe in equality among men, women, and among different cultural heritages. We recognize the importance of a common language. We also follow a civic creed derived from the principles of liberty, equality, democracy, constitutionalism, liberalism, limited government, and private enterprise.

It is our national identity, this sense of nationalism, which promotes democracy, enhances a sense of identity and respect for difference, and enables people to acquire a sense of community that encourages social justice and mutual aid.[35] Nationalism is synonymous with patriotism. Our patriotism, our pride in our national identity "…enhances our sense of self, adds to our enjoyment of difference, increases our possibility of participation in public life, and enriches the world community."[36] From patriotism flows the idea of personal sacrifice for the greater good of the nation. It is this commitment that has allowed us to weather such hardships as the great depression, two world wars, and natural disasters. Through nationalism, we have maintained a society that promotes freedom of expression, ingenuity, and entrepreneurship. In turn, America reaped the benefits of the industrial revolution and economic expansion that we take for granted today. Through nationalism, Americans have pledged their lives and their fortunes to defend our national interests.

The immigrants of the late twentieth and early twenty-first centuries are from Asia, Mexico, Latin America, and the Caribbean. They have come in greater numbers and more quickly than we had experienced in the past. This new generation of immigrants has been harder to integrate than earlier immigrants were because there have been fewer pressures on them to assimilate and learn English. Multiculturism and offspring government programs such as bilingual education, as well as ethnic clustering have hampered the progress of our American melting pot.[37]

In rejecting the melting pot concept, political activists claiming multicultural rights and privileges want to preserve immigrant culture and languages rather than absorb American culture. Such a movement risks the disintegration of our national identity, and paints a picture of a future United States wherein the population consists of competing ethnic groups, all lacking a sense of common culture or political heritage.[38]

What if the United States were to become truly multicultural? We would then be a society in which we no longer have a common culture and national identity. American identity and unity would depend on a continuing consensus on a political ideology derived from a series of negotiations and compromises between competing ethnic groups. How committed would the average American be to a national political ideology bearing little resemblance to his or her own ideology? We as Americans have always viewed our commitment to universal values such as liberty, equality, and individual rights as a great source of national strength. That ideology, Swedish economist Gunnar Myrdal observed, has been "the cement in the structure of this great and disparate nation."[39] In a multicultural America without an underlying common culture and creed, however, national unity would be fragile and unsustainable. The importance of national unity and our common ideology would give way to subnational interests. The foundation of our national political ideology would be built upon a compromised set of principles and values that the average American may not be willing to protect with blood and treasure.

Unlike the United States, political ideology bears little semblance to national identity for most countries. Many great nations over the course of history have come and gone with the fall of their ideologies. China's history is marked by multiple dynasties. European and Middle Eastern countries have all experienced the rise and fall of various ruling ideologies such as those of the Roman and Greek empires, the Persians, the Mongolians, and so on. "The fate of the Soviet Union offers a sobering example for Americans. The United States and the Soviet Union resembled each other in that each defined itself in terms of an ideology. If multiculturalism prevails and if the consensus on liberal democracy disintegrates, the United States could join the Soviet Union on the ash heap of history."[40]

By design, we are not a multicultural nation. What defines our national political ideology is our American culture and creed. What makes our national political ideology endure as a model for the entire world is a history of welcoming new Americans to our country and integrating them into our American culture. "The new Americans of the twenty-first century, like the new Americans of the past, can be interwoven into the fabric of American life. That interweaving is part of the basic character of the country and that the descendants of the new Americans of today can be as much an integral part of their country as the descendants of new Americans of a hundred years ago."[41] The foundation for the interweaving of the next generation of Americans resides in an effective integration program that requires immigrants to learn our language, our civic culture, and become contributing members of our society. All the while, we must also continue to recognize the uniqueness of their heritages, and allow them to retain ties to their culture through customs, religion, and language just as the descendents of the new Americans of the past now enjoy.

President George W. Bush recognized that it is in our national interest to properly integrate immigrants into our society in his comment: "one of the primary reasons America became a great power in the twentieth century is because we welcomed the talent and the character and the patriotism of immigrant families."[42] President Bush's words touch on the underlying impact of our melting pot on our national security. We built our vast industrial base and large economy on the backs, and with the minds, of immigrants. Our successful assimilation of them into our American culture instilled a sense of national identity and pride as well. Immigrants met the call to come to arms and fought side by side with other brave and patriotic Americans when enemies threatened our vital national interests. Without immigrants, and without Americans integrating them into our society so that they also see themselves as American, the United States will not continue to be the great nation it is today. In contrast to the arguments of the proponents of the tossed salad metaphor, our long history of successfully assimilating immigrants into our culture gives proof to the fact that we are an American melting pot.

If history is any indicator of the future, then it is absolutely essential to our national security that we continue our societal melting pot if we are to retain the universal principles contained in our founding documents within our collective psyche. We as Americans have always held our national identity as superior to all other subnational, cultural or ethnic identities. We derive our national interests from our national identity. Our national interests are manifested in our national political ideology,

19

national policies, and in our National Security Strategy. We sustain the continuity of our national political ideology and our national interests by refreshing our society with the integration of newcomers, and melting them into our American society. For without the melting pot, America would truly be lost.

Endnotes

[1] Samuel P. Huntington, "The Erosion of American National Interests," September/October 1997, linked from *Foreign Affairs Home Page* at "Essays," http://www.foreignaffairs.com (accessed November 2, 2011).

[2] Michael Barone, *The New Americans, How The Melting Pot Can Work Again* (Washington, DC: Regnery Publishing, Inc., 2001), 3.

[3] Ibid.

[4] Barbara C. Cruz and Michael J. Berson, "The American Melting Pot? Miscegenation Laws in the United States", http://search.proquest.com.ezproxy.usawcpubs.org/docview/213736384?accountid=4444 (accessed November 2, 2011).

[5] Barone, *The New Americans*, 277.

[6] Peter Duignan, "Do Immigrants Benefit America?," February, 2004, http://search.proquest.com/docview/235846826?accountid=4444 (accessed November 2, 2011).

[7] Samuel P. Huntington, "The Erosion of American National Interests," September/October 1997, linked from *Foreign Affairs Home Page* at "Essays," http://www.foreignaffairs.com (accessed November 2, 2011).

[8] Barone, *The New Americans*, 11.

[9] Samuel P. Huntington, "The Erosion of American National Interests," September/October 1997, linked from *Foreign Affairs Home Page* at "Essays," http://www.foreignaffairs.com (accessed November 2, 2011).

[10] "Saint Frances X. Cabrini," linked from *Immigration Update Home Page* at "famous american immigrants," http://immigrationupdate.wordpress.com/famous-american-immigrants/ (accessed February 6, 2012).

[11] "Saint Frances Xavier Cabrini," linked from Catholic Online Home Page at "Saints," http://www.catholic.org/saints/ (accessed February 7, 2012).

[12] "George Washington Carver," linked from *The Black Collegian Online Archives Home Page* at "African American History," http://www.black-collegian.com/african/aaprofil.shtm (accessed February 6, 2012).

[13] "George Washington Carver," linked from *Biography Home Page* at "people," http://www.biography.com/people/george-washington-carver-9240299 (accessed February 7, 2012).

[14] "Madeleine Albright," linked from *Immigration Update Home Page* at "famous american immigrants," http://immigrationupdate.wordpress.com/famous-american-immigrants/ (accessed February 6, 2012).

[15] "Madeleine Albright," linked from *Biography Home Page* at "people," http://www.biography.com/people/madeleine-albright-9179300 (accessed February 7, 2012).

[16] Peter Duignan, "Do Immigrants Benefit America?," February, 2004, http://search.proquest.com/docview/235846826?accountid=4444 (accessed November 2, 2011).

[17] Barone, *The New Americans*, 12.

[18] Samuel P. Huntington, "The Erosion of American National Interests," September/October 1997, linked from *Foreign Affairs Home Page* at "Essays," http://www.foreignaffairs.com (accessed November 2, 2011).

[19] Ibid.

[20] Barone, *The New Americans*, 13.

[21] David M. Haugen, Susan Musser, and Kacy Lovelace, eds., *Immigration*, Opposing Viewpoints Series (Farmington Hills: Greenhaven Press, 2009), 76.

[22] Ibid.

[23] Ibid., 77.

[24] Ibid., 82.

[25] Ibid., 66.

[26] Ibid., 65,66.

[27] Ibid., 68.

[28] Ibid., 67.

[29] Charles P. Cozic, ed., *NATIONALISM AND ETHNIC CONFLICT*, Current Controversies Series (San Diego: Greenhaven Press, 1994), 46.

[30] John Fetto, "An All-American Melting Pot," July, 2001, http://search.proquest.com.ezproxy.usawcpubs.org/pagepdf/200631301/fulltextPDF?accountid= 4444 (accessed November 2, 2011).

[31] Ibid.

[32] Ibid.

[33] Ibid.

[34] Ibid.

[35] Charles P. Cozic, ed., *NATIONALISM AND ETHNIC CONFLICT*, 26.

[36] Ibid, 33.

[37] Peter Duignan, "Do Immigrants Benefit America?," February, 2004, http://search.proquest.com/docview/235846826?accountid=4444 (accessed November 2, 2011).

[38] Ibid.

[39] Samuel P. Huntington, "The Erosion of American National Interests," September/October 1997, linked from *Foreign Affairs Home Page* at "Essays," http://www.foreignaffairs.com (accessed November 2, 2011).

[40] Ibid.

[41] Barone, *The New Americans*, 279.

[42] David M. Haugen, Susan Musser, and Kacy Lovelace, eds., *Immigration*, 200.